The Key Facts™ on

Germany

Essential Information on Germany

By Patrick W. Nee

The Internationalist®
www.internationalist.com

The Internationalist®

International Business, Investment, and Travel

Published by:

The Internationalist Publishing Company

96 Walter Street/ Suite 200

Boston, MA 02131, USA

Tel: 617-354-7722

www.internationalist.com

PN@internationalist.com

Copyright © 2015 by PWN

09092015

The Internationalist is a Registered Trademark. "Key Facts" and "The Internationalist Business Guides" are Trademarks of The Internationalist Publishing Company.

All Rights are reserved under International, Pan-American, and Pan-Asian Conventions. No part of this book may be reproduced in any form without the written permission of the publisher. All rights vigorously enforced

Table Of Contents

Chapter 1: Background:

As Europe's largest economy and second most populous nation (after Russia), Germany is a key member of the continent's economic, political, and defense organizations. European power struggles immersed Germany in two devastating World Wars in the first half of the 20th century and left the country occupied by the victorious Allied powers of the US, UK, France, and the Soviet Union in 1945. With the advent of the Cold War, two German states were formed in 1949: the western Federal Republic of Germany (FRG) and the eastern German Democratic Republic (GDR). The democratic FRG embedded itself in key Western economic and security organizations, the EC, which became the EU, and NATO, while the Communist GDR was on the front line of the Soviet-led Warsaw Pact. The decline of the USSR and the end of the Cold War allowed for German unification in 1990. Since then, Germany has expended considerable funds to bring Eastern productivity and wages up to Western standards. In January 1999, Germany and 10 other EU countries introduced a common European exchange currency, the euro.

Chapter 2: Geography

Location:

Central Europe, bordering the Baltic Sea and the North Sea, between the Netherlands and Poland, south of Denmark

Geographic coordinates:

51 00 N, 9 00 E

Map references:

Europe

Area:

total: 357,022 sq km

country comparison to the world: 63

land: 348,672 sq km

water: 8,350 sq km

Area - comparative:

slightly smaller than Montana

Land boundaries:

total: 3,790 km

border countries: Austria 801 km, Belgium 133 km, Czech Republic 704 km, Denmark 140 km, France 418 km, Luxembourg 128 km, Netherlands 575 km, Poland 467 km, Switzerland 348 km

Coastline:

2,389 km

Maritime claims:

    territorial sea: 12 nm

    exclusive economic zone: 200 nm

    continental shelf: 200 m depth or to the depth of

    exploitation

Climate:

    temperate and marine; cool, cloudy, wet winters and

    summers; occasional warm mountain (foehn) wind

Terrain:

    lowlands in north, uplands in center, Bavarian Alps in

south

Elevation extremes:

    lowest point: Neuendorf bei Wilster -3.54 m

    highest point: Zugspitze 2,963 m

Natural resources:

    coal, lignite, natural gas, iron ore, copper, nickel,

    uranium, potash, salt, construction materials, timber,

    arable land

Land use:

    arable land: 34.1%

    permanent crops: 0.6%

    other: 65.3% (2011 est.)

Irrigated land:

    5,157 sq km (2006)

Total renewable water resources:

    154 cu km (2011)

Freshwater withdrawal (domestic/industrial/agricultural):

total: 32.3 cu km/yr (16%/84%/0%)

per capita: 391.4 cu m/yr (2007)

Natural hazards:

flooding

Environment - current issues:

emissions from coal-burning utilities and industries contribute to air pollution; acid rain, resulting from sulfur dioxide emissions, is damaging forests; pollution in the Baltic Sea from raw sewage and industrial effluents from rivers in eastern Germany; hazardous waste disposal; government established a mechanism for ending the use of nuclear power over the next 15 years; government working to meet EU commitment to identify nature preservation areas in line with the EU's Flora, Fauna, and Habitat directive

Environment - international agreements:

party to: Air Pollution, Air Pollution-Nitrogen Oxides, Air Pollution-Persistent Organic Pollutants, Air Pollution-Sulfur 85, Air Pollution-Sulfur 94, Air Pollution-Volatile Organic Compounds, Antarctic-Environmental Protocol, Antarctic-Marine Living Resources, Antarctic Seals, Antarctic Treaty, Biodiversity, Climate Change, Climate Change-Kyoto Protocol, Desertification, Endangered Species, Environmental Modification, Hazardous Wastes, Law of the Sea, Marine Dumping, Ozone Layer Protection, Ship Pollution, Tropical Timber 83, Tropical Timber 94, Wetlands, Whaling

signed, but not ratified: none of the selected agreements

Geography - note:

strategic location on North European Plain and along the entrance to the Baltic Sea

Chapter 3: People and Society

Nationality:

noun: German(s)

adjective: German

Ethnic groups:

German 91.5%, Turkish 2.4%, other 6.1% (made up largely of Greek, Italian, Polish, Russian, Serbo-Croatian, Spanish)

Languages:

German

Religions:

Protestant 34%, Roman Catholic 34%, Muslim 3.7%, unaffiliated or other 28.3%

Population:

80,854,408 (July 2015 est.)

country comparison to the world: 18

Age structure:

0-14 years: 12.88% (male 5,346,086/female 5,068,071)

15-24 years: 10.38% (male 4,279,962/female 4,113,746)

25-54 years: 41.38% (male 16,934,180/female 16,519,932)

55-64 years: 13.91% (male 5,571,694/female 5,675,104)

65 years and over: 21.45% (male 7,591,298/female 9,754,335) (2015 est.)

Median age:

> total: 46.1 years
>
> male: 45.1 years
>
> female: 47.2 years (2014 est.)

Population growth rate:

> -0.17% (2015 est.)
>
> country comparison to the world: 212

Birth rate:

> 8.47 births/1,000 population (2015 est.)
>
> country comparison to the world: 219

Death rate:

> 11.42 deaths/1,000 population (2015 est.)
>
> country comparison to the world: 31

Net migration rate:

> 1.24 migrant(s)/1,000 population (2015 est.)
>
> country comparison to the world: 60

Urbanization:

> urban population: 75.3% of total population (2015)
>
> rate of urbanization: 0.16% annual rate of change (2010-
> 15 est.)

Major cities - population:

> BERLIN (capital) 3.563 million; Hamburg 1.831 million;
> Munich 1.438 million; Cologne 1.037 million (2015)

Sex ratio:

> at birth: 1.06 male(s)/female
>
> under 15 years: 1.05 male(s)/female

15-64 years: 1.02 male(s)/female

65 years and over: 0.78 male(s)/female

total population: 0.97 male(s)/female (2015 est.)

Infant mortality rate:

total: 3.43 deaths/1,000 live births

country comparison to the world: 209

male: 3.72 deaths/1,000 live births

female: 3.12 deaths/1,000 live births (2015 est.)

Life expectancy at birth:

total population: 80.57 years

country comparison to the world: 28

male: 78.26 years

female: 83 years (2015 est.)

Total fertility rate:

1.44 children born/woman (2015 est.)

country comparison to the world: 209

Health expenditures:

11.3% of GDP (2013)

country comparison to the world: 13

Physicians density:

3.89 physicians/1,000 population (2012)

Hospital bed density:

8.2 beds/1,000 population (2011)

Sanitation facility access:

improved:

urban: 100% of population

rural: 100% of population

total: 100% of population

HIV/AIDS - adult prevalence rate:

0.15% (2013 est.)

country comparison to the world: 102

HIV/AIDS - people living with HIV/AIDS:

77,500 (2013 est.)

country comparison to the world: 102

HIV/AIDS - deaths:

400 (2013 est.)

country comparison to the world: 88

Obesity - adult prevalence rate:

22.7% (2014)

country comparison to the world: 59

Children under the age of 5 years underweight:

1.1% (2006)

country comparison to the world: 132

Education expenditures:

5% of GDP (2011)

country comparison to the world: 74

Literacy:

definition: age 15 and over can read and write

total population: 99%

male: 99%

female: 99% (2003 est.)

School life expectancy (primary to tertiary education):

total: 16 years

male: 17 years

female: 16 years (2012)

Unemployment, youth ages 15-24:

total: 8.1%

country comparison to the world: 112

male: 8.8%

female: 7.4% (2009)

Chapter 4: Government

Country name:

conventional long form: Federal Republic of Germany

conventional short form: Germany

local long form: Bundesrepublik Deutschland

local short form: Deutschland

former: German Empire, German Republic, German Reich

Government type:

federal republic

Capital:

name: Berlin

geographic coordinates: 52 31 N, 13 24 E

time difference: UTC+1 (6 hours ahead of Washington, DC during Standard Time)

daylight saving time: +1hr, begins last Sunday in March; ends last Sunday in October

Administrative divisions:

16 states (Laender, singular - Land); Baden-Wuerttemberg, Bayern (Bavaria), Berlin, Brandenburg, Bremen, Hamburg, Hessen (Hesse), Mecklenburg-Vorpommern (Mecklenburg-Western Pomerania), Niedersachsen (Lower Saxony), Nordrhein-Westfalen (North Rhine-Westphalia), Rheinland-Pfalz (Rhineland-Palatinate), Saarland, Sachsen (Saxony), Sachsen-Anhalt

(Saxony-Anhalt), Schleswig-Holstein, Thueringen (Thuringia); note - Bayern, Sachsen, and Thueringen refer to themselves as free states (Freistaaten, singular - Freistaat), while Hamburg prides itself on being a Free and Hanseatic City (Freie und Hansestadt)

Independence:

18 January 1871 (German Empire unification); divided into four zones of occupation (UK, US, USSR, and France) in 1945 following World War II; Federal Republic of Germany (FRG or West Germany) proclaimed on 23 May 1949 and included the former UK, US, and French zones; German Democratic Republic (GDR or East Germany) proclaimed on 7 October 1949 and included the former USSR zone; West Germany and East Germany unified on 3 October 1990; all four powers formally relinquished rights on 15 March 1991; notable earlier dates: 10 August 843 (Eastern Francia established from the division of the Carolingian Empire); 2 February 962 (crowning of OTTO I, recognized as the first Holy Roman Emperor)

National holiday:

Unity Day, 3 October (1990)

Constitution:

previous 1919 (Weimar Constitution); latest drafted 10 to 23 August 1948, approved 12 May 1949, promulgated

23 May 1949, entered into force 24 May 1949; amended
many times, last in 2012 (2012)

Legal system:

civil law system

International law organization participation:

accepts compulsory ICJ jurisdiction with reservations;
accepts ICCt jurisdiction

Suffrage:

18 years of age; universal

Executive branch:

chief of state: President Joachim GAUCK (since 23
March 2012)

head of government: Chancellor Angela MERKEL
(since 22 November 2005)

cabinet: Cabinet or Bundesminister (Federal Ministers)
appointed by the president on the recommendation of the
chancellor

elections: president indirectly elected for a 5-year term
(eligibel for a second term) by a Federal Convention
consisting of the 630-member Federal Parliament
(Bundestag) and 630 delegates indirectly elected by the
state parliaments; election last held on 19 February 2012
(next to be held by June 2017); chancellor indirectly
elected by absolute majority by the Federal parliament
for a 4-year term; Federal parliament vote for chancellor

last held on 17 December 2013 (next to be held following the September 2017 general election)

<u>election results</u>: Joachim GAUCK elected president; Federal Convention vote count – Joachim GAUCK (independent) 991, Beate KLARSFELD (independent) 126, Olaf ROSE (National People's Union) 3; Angela MERKEL (CDU) reelcted chancellor; Federal Parliament vote – 462 for, 150 against, 4 abstentions

Legislative branch:

<u>bicameral Parliament (Parlament)</u> consists of the Federael council or Bundesrat (69 seats; members appointed by each of the 16 state governments or landtags) and the Federal Diet or Bundestag (631 seats – total seats can vary each electoral term; approximately one-half of members directly elected in multi-seat constituencies by proportional representation vote and approximately one-half directly elected in single-seat constituencies by simple majority vote; members serve 4-year terms)

<u>elections</u>: Bundestag – last held on 22 September 2013 (next to be held no later than autumn 2017); most all postwar German governments have been coalitions; note – there are no elections for the Bundesrat; composition is detemined by the composition of the state-level governments; the composition of the Bundesrat has the

potential to change any time one of the 16 states holds an election

election results: Bundestag – percent of vote by party – CDU/CSU 41.5%, SPD 25.7%, Left 8.6%, Greens 8.4%, FDP 4.8%, other 10.9%; seats by party – CDU/CSU 311, SPD 193, Left 64, Greens 63

Judicial branch:

Federal Constitutional Court or Bundesverfassungsgericht (half the judges are elected by the Bundestag and half by the Bundesrat); Federal Court of Justice; Federal Administrative Court

Political parties and leaders:

Alliance '90/Greens [Cem OEZDEMIR and Simone PETER];Alternative for Germany or AfD [Bernd LUCKE]; Christian Democratic Union or CDU [Angela MERKEL]; Christian Social Union or CSU [Horst SEEHOFER]; Free Democratic Party or FDP [Christian LINDNER]; Left Party or Die Linke [Katia KIPPING and Bernd RIEXINGER]; Social Democratic Party or SPD [Sigmar GABRIEL]

Political pressure groups and leaders:

business associations and employers' organizations; trade unions; religious, immigrant, expellee, and veterans groups

International organization participation:

ADB (nonregional member), AfDB (nonregional member), Arctic Council (observer), Australia Group, BIS, BSEC (observer), CBSS, CD, CDB, CE, CERN, EAPC, EBRD, ECB, EIB, EITI (implementing country), EMU, ESA, EU, FAO, FATF, G-5, G-7, G-8, G-10, G-20, IADB, IAEA, IBRD, ICAO, ICC (national committees), ICCt, ICRM, IDA, IEA, IFAD, IFC, IFRCS, IGAD (partners), IHO, ILO, IMF, IMO, IMSO, Interpol, IOC, IOM, IPU, ISO, ITSO, ITU, ITUC (NGOs), MIGA, MINURSO, NATO, NEA, NSG, OAS (observer), OECD, OPCW, OSCE, Pacific Alliance (observer), Paris Club, PCA, Schengen Convention, SELEC (observer), SICA (observer), UN, UNAMID, UNCTAD, UNESCO, UNHCR, UNIDO, UNIFIL, UNMISS, UNRWA, UNSC (temporary), UNWTO, UPU, WCO, WHO, WIPO, WMO, WTO, ZC

Diplomatic representation in the US:

chief of mission: Ambassador Hans Peter WITTIG (since 21 May 2014)

chancery: 4645 Reservoir Road NW, Washington, DC 20007

telephone: [1] (202) 298-4000

FAX: [1] (202) 298-4249

consulate(s) general: Atlanta, Boston, Chicago, Houston, Los Angeles, Miami, New York, San Francisco

Diplomatic representation from the US:

chief of mission: Ambassador Hans Peter WITTIG

(since 21 May 2014)

embassy: Pariser Platz 2

mailing address: Clayallee 170, 14191 Berlin

telephone: [49] (30) 8305-0

FAX: [49] (30) 8305-1215

consulate(s) general: Duesseldorf, Frankfurt am Main,

Hamburg, Leipzig, Munich

Key Leaders:

Fed. Pres.	**Joachim GAUCK**
Chancellor	**Angela MERKEL**
Vice Chancellor	**Sigmar GABRIEL**
Min. of Defense	**Ursula VON DER LEYEN**
Min. for Economic Cooperation & Development	**Gerd MUELLER**
Min. for Economics & Energy	**Sigmar GABRIEL**
Min. for Education & Research	**Johanna WANKA**
Min. for the Environment, Nature Conservation, Construction, & Reactor Security	**Barbara HENDRICKS**
Min. for Family, Seniors, Women, & Youth	**Manuela SCHWESIG**
Min. of Finance	**Wolfgang**

	SCHAEUBLE
Min. of Foreign Affairs	Frank-Walter STEINMEIER
Min. for Health	Hermann GROEHE
Min. of Interior	Thomas DE MAIZIERE
Min. of Justice & Consumer Protection	Heiko MAAS
Min. for Labor & Social Affairs	Andrea NAHLES
Min. for Transportation & Digital Infrastructure	Alexander DOBRINDT
Min. Without Portfolio & Chancellery Chief	Peter ALTMAIER
Pres., Bundesbank	Jens WEIDMANN
Ambassador to the US	Peter WITTIG
Permanent Representative to the UN, New York	Harald BRAUN

Flag description:

three equal horizontal bands of black (top), red, and gold; these colors have played an important role in German history and can be traced back to the medieval banner of the Holy Roman Emperor - a black eagle with red claws and beak on a gold field

National symbol(s):

black eagle

National anthem:

name: "Lied der Deutschen" (Song of the Germans)

lyrics/music: August Heinrich HOFFMANN VON FALLERSLEBEN/Franz Joseph HAYDN

note: adopted 1922, restored 1990; the anthem, also known as "Deutschlandlied" (Song of Germany), was abolished in 1945 because of the Nazi's use of the first verse, specifically the phrase, "Deutschland, Deutschland ueber alles" (Germany, Germany above all) to promote nationalism; since restoration in 1990, only the third verse is sung

Chapter 5: Economy

Overview:

The German economy - the fifth largest economy in the world in PPP terms and Europe's largest - is a leading exporter of machinery, vehicles, chemicals, and household equipment and benefits from a highly skilled labor force. Like its Western European neighbors, Germany faces significant demographic challenges to sustained long-term growth. Low fertility rates and declining net immigration are increasing pressure on the country's social welfare system and necessitate structural reforms. Reforms launched by the government of Chancellor Gerhard SCHROEDER (1998-2005), deemed necessary to address chronically high unemployment and low average growth, contributed to strong growth in 2006 and 2007 and falling unemployment. These advances, as well as a government subsidized, reduced working hour scheme, help explain the relatively modest increase in unemployment during the 2008-09 recession - the deepest since World War II - and its decrease to 5.2% in 2014. The new German government introduced a minimum wage of about $11.60 (8.50 euros) per hour to take effect in 2015. Stimulus and stabilization efforts initiated in 2008 and 2009 and tax cuts introduced in Chancellor Angela

MERKEL's second term increased Germany's total budget deficit – in 2011 and in 2012 Germany reached a budget surplus of 0.1%. The budget was essentially in balance in 2014. A constitutional amendment approved in 2009 limits the federal government to structural deficits of no more than 0.35% of GDP per annum as of 2016 though the target was already reached in 2012. The German economy suffers from low levels of investment, and a government plan to invest 15 billion euros 2016-18, largely in infrastructure, is intended to spur needed private investment. Following the March 2011 Fukushima nuclear disaster, Chancellor Angela MERKEL announced in May 2011 that eight of the country's 17 nuclear reactors would be shut down immediately and the remaining plants would close by 2022. Germany plans to replace nuclear power with renewable energy, which accounted for 27.8% of gross electricity consumption in 2014, up from 9% in 2000. Before the shutdown of the eight reactors, Germany relied on nuclear power for 23% of its electricity generationg capacity and 46% of its base-load electricity production. Extremely low inflation, caused largely by low global energy prices and a weak euro, are expected to boost german GDP growth in 2015.

GDP (purchasing power parity):

$3.722 trillion (2014 est.)

country comparison to the world: 6

$3.633 trillion (2013 est.)

$3.655 trillion (2012 est.)

note: data are in 2014 US dollars

GDP (official exchange rate):

$3.86 trillion (2014 est.)

GDP - real growth rate:

1.6% (2014 est.)

country comparison to the world: 165

0.2% (2013 est.)

0.6% (2012 est.)

GDP - per capita (PPP):

$45,900 (2014 est.)

country comparison to the world: 27

$45,200 (2013 est.)

$45,100 (2012 est.)

note: data are in 2014 US dollars

GDP - composition by sector:

agriculture: 0.9%

industry: 30.8%

services: 68.4% (2014 est.)

Labor force:

42.65 million (2014 est.)

country comparison to the world: 15

Labor force - by occupation:

agriculture: 1.6%

industry: 24.6%

services: 73.8% (2011)

Unemployment rate:

5% (2014 est.)

country comparison to the world: 49

5.3% (2013 est.)

Population below poverty line:

15.5% (2010 est.)

Household income or consumption by percentage share:

lowest 10%: 3.6%

highest 10%: 24% (2000)

Distribution of family income - Gini index:

27 (2006)

country comparison to the world: 129

30 (1994)

Investment (gross fixed):

20.2% of GDP (2014 est.)

Budget:

revenues: $1.68 trillion

expenditures: $1.664 trillion (2014 est.)

Taxes and other revenues:

44% of GDP (2014 est.)

country comparison to the world: 27

Budget surplus (+) or deficit (-):

0.4% of GDP (2014 est.)

country comparison to the world: 33

Public debt:

74.7% of GDP (2014 est.)

country comparison to the world: 33

76.9% of GDP (2013 est.)

note: general government gross debt is defined in the Maastricht Treaty as consolidated general government gross debt at nominal value, outstanding at the end of the year in the following categories of government liabilities (as defined in ESA95): currency and deposits (AF.2), securities other than shares excluding financial derivatives (AF.3, excluding AF.34), and loans (AF.4); the general government sector comprises the sub-sectors of central government, state government, local government and social security funds; the series are presented as a percentage of GDP and in millions of euro; GDP used as a denominator is the gross domestic product at current market prices; data expressed in national currency are converted into euro using end-year exchange rates provided by the European Central Bank

Inflation rate (consumer prices):

0.8% (2014 est.)

country comparison to the world: 53

1.5% (2013 est.)

Central bank discount rate:

0.75% (31 December 2013)

country comparison to the world: 128

1.5% (31 December 2010)

note: this is the European Central Bank's rate on the marginal lending facility, which offers overnight credit to banks in the euro area

Commercial bank prime lending rate:

2.6% (31 December 2014 est.)

country comparison to the world: 178

2.76% (31 December 2013 est.)

Stock of narrow money:

$2.236 trillion (31 December 2014 est.)

country comparison to the world: 5

$2.244 trillion (31 December 2013 est.)

note: see entry for the European Union for money supply in the euro area; the European Central Bank (ECB) controls monetary policy for the 17 members of the Economic and Monetary Union (EMU); individual members of the EMU do not control the quantity of money circulating within their own borders

Stock of broad money:

$4.347 trillion (31 December 2014 est.)

country comparison to the world: 5

$4.451 trillion (31 December 2013 est.)

Stock of domestic credit:

$4.253 trillion (31 December 2012 est.)

country comparison to the world: 5

$4.188 trillion (31 December 2011 est.)

Market value of publicly traded shares:

$1.486 trillion (31 December 2012 est.)

country comparison to the world: 9

$1.184 trillion (31 December 2011)

$1.43 trillion (31 December 2010)

Agriculture - products:

potatoes, wheat, barley, sugar beets, fruit, cabbages; cattle, pigs, poultry

Industrial production growth rate:

1.3% (2014 est.)

country comparison to the world: 145

Current account balance:

$287.5 billion (2014 est.)

country comparison to the world: 1

$274 billion (2013 est.)

Exports:

$1.547 trillion (2014 est.)

country comparison to the world: 4

$1.506 trillion (2013 est.)

Exports - commodities:

motor vehicles, machinery, chemicals, computer and electronic products, electrical equipment, pharmaceuticals, metals, transport equipment, foodstuffs, textiles, rubber and plastic products

Imports:

$1.319 trillion (2014 est.)

country comparison to the world: 4

$1.249 trillion (2013 est.)

Imports - commodities:

machinery, data processing equipment, vehicles, chemicals, oil and gas, metals, electric equipment, pharmaceuticals, foodstuffs, agricultural products

Reserves of foreign exchange and gold:

$198.2 billion (31 December 2013 est.)

country comparison to the world: 14

Debt - external:

$5.624 trillion (30 June 2011)

country comparison to the world: 5

$4.713 trillion (30 June 2010)

Stock of direct foreign investment - at home:

$1.424 trillion (31 December 2014 est.)

country comparison to the world: 4

$1.384 billion (31 December 2013 est.)

Stock of direct foreign investment - abroad:

$2.048 trillion (31 December 2014 est.)

<u>country comparison to the world</u>: 2

$1.971 trillion (31 December 2013 est.)

Exchange rates:

euros (EUR) per US dollar –

0.7489 (2014 est.)

0.7634 (2013 est.)

0.78 (2012 est.)

0.7185 (2011 est.)

0.755 (2010 est.)

Fiscal year:

calendar year

Chapter 6: Energy

Electricity - production:

    575.9 billion kWh (2012 est.)

    country comparison to the world: 8

Electricity - consumption:

    582.5 billion kWh (2012 est.)

    country comparison to the world: 7

Electricity - exports:

    57.92 billion kWh (2010 est.)

    country comparison to the world: 3

Electricity - imports:

    71.43 billion kWh (2013 est.)

    country comparison to the world: 2

Electricity - installed generating capacity:

    178.4 million kW (2012 est.)

    country comparison to the world: 6

Electricity - from fossil fuels:

    51% of total installed capacity (2012 est.)

    country comparison to the world: 6

Electricity - from nuclear fuels:

    7% of total installed capacity (2012 est.)

    country comparison to the world: 22

Electricity - from hydroelectric plants:

    6% of total installed capacity (2012 est.)

    country comparison to the world: 22

Electricity - from other renewable sources:

36% of total installed capacity (2012 est.)

country comparison to the world: 3

Crude oil - production:

97,000 bbl/day (2013 est.)

country comparison to the world: 49

Crude oil - exports:

3,907 bbl/day (2012 est.)

country comparison to the world: 64

Crude oil - imports:

1.881 million bbl/day (2012 est.)

country comparison to the world: 6

Crude oil - proved reserves:

232.6 million bbl (1 January 2014 est.)

country comparison to the world: 57

Refined petroleum products - production:

2.206 million bbl/day (2012 est.)

country comparison to the world: 8

Refined petroleum products - consumption:

2.403 million bbl/day (2013 est.)

country comparison to the world: 9

Refined petroleum products - exports:

376,600 bbl/day (2012 est.)

country comparison to the world: 19

Refined petroleum products - imports:

666,300 bbl/day (2010 est.)

country comparison to the world: 10

Natural gas - production:

11.78 billion cu m (2013 est.)

country comparison to the world: 41

Natural gas - consumption:

88.44 billion cu m (2013 est.)

country comparison to the world: 9

Natural gas - exports:

18.82 billion cu m (2013 est.)

country comparison to the world: 15

Natural gas - imports:

94.91 billion cu m (2013 est.)

country comparison to the world: 3

Natural gas - proved reserves:

116 billion cu m (1 January 2014 est.)

country comparison to the world: 50

Carbon dioxide emissions from consumption of energy:

788.3 million Mt (2012 est.)

country comparison to the world: 7

Chapter 7: Communications

Telephones - main lines in use:

47.02 million (2014)

country comparison to the world: 5

Telephones - mobile cellular:

99.5 million (2014)

country comparison to the world: 15

Telephone system:

general assessment: Germany has one of the world's most technologically advanced telecommunications systems; as a result of intensive capital expenditures since reunification, the formerly backward system of the eastern part of the country, dating back to World War II, has been modernized and integrated with that of the western part

domestic: Germany is served by an extensive system of automatic telephone exchanges connected by modern networks of fiber-optic cable, coaxial cable, microwave radio relay, and a domestic satellite system; cellular telephone service is widely available, expanding rapidly, and includes roaming service to many foreign countries

international: country code - 49; Germany's international service is excellent worldwide, consisting of extensive land and undersea cable facilities as well as earth

stations in the Inmarsat, Intelsat, Eutelsat, and
Intersputnik satellite systems (2011)

Broadcast media:

a mixture of publicly-operated and privately-owned TV
and radio stations; national and regional public
broadcasters compete with nearly 400 privately-owned
national and regional TV stations; more than 90% of
households have cable or satellite TV; hundreds of radio
stations including multiple national radio networks,
regional radio networks, and a large number of local
radio stations (2008)

Internet country code:

.de

Internet users:

70.3 million (2014 est.)

country comparison to the world: 8

Chapter 8: Transportation

Airports:

    539 (2013)

    country comparison to the world: 13

Airports - with paved runways:

    total: 318

    over 3,047 m: 14

    2,438 to 3,047 m: 49

    1,524 to 2,437 m: 60

    914 to 1,523 m: 70

    under 914 m: 125 (2012)

Airports - with unpaved runways:

    total: 221

    1,524 to 2,437 m: 1

    914 to 1,523 m: 35

    under 914 m: 185 (2013)

Heliports:

    23 (2013)

Pipelines:

    gas 26,985 km; oil 2,826 km; refined products 4,479 km
(2010)

Railways:

    total: 43,468.3 km

    country comparison to the world: 6

standard gauge: 43,209.3 km 1.435-m gauge (19,973 km electrified)

narrow gauge: 220 km 1.000-m gauge (79 km electrified); 15 km 0.900-m gauge; 24 km 0.750-m gauge (2014)

Roadways:

total: 645,000 km

country comparison to the world: 11

paved: 645,000 km (includes 12,800 km of expressways)

note: includes local roads (2010)

Waterways:

7,467 km (Rhine River carries most goods; Main-Danube Canal links North Sea and Black Sea) (2012)

country comparison to the world: 18

Merchant marine:

total: 427

country comparison to the world: 24

by type: barge carrier 2, bulk carrier 6, cargo 51, carrier 1, chemical tanker 15, container 298, liquefied gas 6, passenger 4, passenger/cargo 24, petroleum tanker 10, refrigerated cargo 3, roll on/roll off 6, vehicle carrier 1

foreign-owned: 6 (Finland 3, Netherlands 1, Switzerland 2)

registered in other countries: 3,420 (Antigua and Barbuda 1094, Australia 2, Bahamas 30, Bermuda 14, Brazil 6, Bulgaria 12, Burma 1, Cayman Islands 3, Cook

Islands 1, Curacao 25, Cyprus 192, Denmark 9, Dominica 5, Estonia 1, France 1, Gibraltar 123, Hong Kong 10, Isle of Man 56, Jamaica 10, Liberia 1185, Luxembourg 9, Malta 135, Marshall Islands 248, Morocco 1, Netherlands 86, NZ 2, Panama 24, Papua New Guinea 1, Philippines 2, Portugal 14, Saint Vincent and the Grenadines 3, Singapore 32, Slovakia 3, Spain 4, Sri Lanka 8, Sweden 3, UK 59, US 5, Venezuela 1) (2010)

Ports and terminals:

Bremen, Bremerhaven, Duisburg, Hamburg, Karlsruhe, Lubeck, Neuss-Dusseldorf

oil terminals: Brunsbuttel Canal terminals

Chapter 9: Military.

Military branches:

Federal Armed Forces (Bundeswehr): Army (Heer), Navy (Deutsche Marine, includes naval air arm), Air Force (Luftwaffe), Joint Support Services (Streitkraeftbasis), Central Medical Service (Zentraler Sanitaetsdienst) (2013)

Military service age and obligation:

17-23 years of age for male and female voluntary military service; conscription ended 1 July 2011; service obligation 8-23 months or 12 years; women have been eligible for voluntary service in all military branches and positions since 2001 (2013)

Manpower available for military service:

males age 16-49: 18,529,299

females age 16-49: 17,888,543 (2010 est.)

Manpower fit for military service:

males age 16-49: 15,027,886

females age 16-49: 14,510,527 (2010 est.)

Manpower reaching militarily significant age annually:

male: 405,438

female: 384,930 (2010 est.)

Military expenditures:

1.35% of GDP (2012 est.)

country comparison to the world: 74

Chapter 10: Transnational Issues

Disputes - international:

Illicit drugs:

source of precursor chemicals for South American cocaine processors; transshipment point for and consumer of Southwest Asian heroin, Latin American cocaine, and European-produced synthetic drugs; major financial center

www.ingramcontent.com/pod-product-compliance
Lightning Source LLC
Chambersburg PA
CBHW051300170526
45165CB00004B/1790